PRAYERS OF FORGIVENESS

Judaism

America Selby

Ladies Image Publishing

Email: americaselby@outlook.com

Ladies Image Publishing

Email: admin@myamazonauthor.com

Dear Reader,

If you enjoyed this book or found it useful, I would be very grateful if you would post a short review on Amazon. Your support really does make a difference and I read all the reviews personally so I can get your feedback and make this book even better.

If you would like to leave a review, all you need to do is click the review link on this book's Amazon page here.

If you are a member of kindleunlimited, I would be most grateful if you would scroll to the back of the book so I will be paid for your borrowed book.

Thanks again for your support.

America Selby

TABLE OF CONTENTS

PRAYER
Help Me Remember Mashiach

INTRODUCTION

Forgive Me for My Prideful Ways

Pride. It causes us to look our best, do our best and be our best, then insults the looks, work and character of our fellow. It warms our hearts as we applaud the accomplishments of a loved one, then casts us into deep depression when we ourselves have not succeeded. Pride is good and evil; it's the motive of our greatest successes and bane of our worst failures. The Bible has much to say about the negative effects of pride. It urges us to go our own way, to plan our own path and in the end; it leads us to destruction. Many misquote the passage found in Proverbs 16:18. It speaks of pride as preceding destruction; not a fall. Pride goes before utter destruction. It destroys those around us when we direct its forces against them, but also rises to destroy us either through self-gratifying boastfulness and striving or through self-condemnation, when the prideful expressions of others are received.

In Judaism, negative pride is seen as an attitude of superiority in the face of God or man. Since we are created by God and made in His image, we are but a slight and insignificant duplication of the real thing. We have no upper hand against the One who originated our existence. He is eminent over all and is in all. Nothing created is ever greater than its creator. Pride before God is at best laughable and at worst futile. The Jewish soul recognizes its utter dependency upon God for all of life. It is God who created us and not we ourselves. We have nothing that He has not given and can do nothing against His hand. We look to Him in our feebleness of existence and He takes mercy. This demonstrates His power and preeminence. He sees our failings and attends to our lowly estate.

When it comes to our fellow man, he stands on the same level as we; each being created by the same God and imbued with a portion of His divine nature. None is better than the other. All men, having been given life and breath from the same creator and each having his days determined by the same, has nothing to boast. In Judaism, we look to the good of our fellow Jew, without insult or injury, and afford the same to all mankind. To rise up in pride against another human being is to rise in the face of God. When met with pride, we are to respond as best as possible without reacting in kind. This is a perpetual difficulty for all. However, there is forgiveness when we recognize our error.

The opposite of pride is humility; thus humility becomes the focal point of our prayer. God will forgive our pride. He knows we are imperfect and prone to an entire litany of self–centered, self-elevating and self-aggrandizing thoughts, words and behaviors. At times, pride arises from personal rejection, embarrassments or hurtful insults, while at others it reveals itself when we

least expect it. Whenever possible, we must rethink and retract every bit of it as it pertains to our fellowman and bow the knee before God.

PRAYER
Forgive Me for my Prideful Ways

Avinu Malkeinu, our Father and our King, forgive us for the sin of pride. May we humbly bow the knee before you and acknowledge that we are but dust with which you have formed us. Cause our gaze to be steadfast toward you as a servant before his master and a subject before his king. Forgive our insolence and create in us a disposition of humility before you and our fellow. Forgive us for haughtiness of eye and tongue and for deeds which have wounded and brought low the soul of another, even our own. Cause us to preserve, with sincerity, the cause of our brother and to uphold his merit with honesty. Revive us with your truth and let not the inclination of evil rule over us in pride.

Be exalted, Oh Lord, above the heavens and may your glory be over the earth which you have wrought. Who is like you among the gods? Who is like you? There is none beside and with none is your glory shared. May you alone be exalted. Not us, Oh Lord, not us. Turn to us, hear us and forgive. Forgive for the sake of your glory. Forgive for the sake of your great name. Forgive us for the sin of pride.

Where we have wounded; let us heal. Where we have injured; let us renew. Where we have been amiss; let us rectify. Let not pride and haughtiness rule over us but your justice, peace, compassion and loving kindness which you bestow toward all men. Let us perform our deeds before you in all humility and regard the wellbeing of all as needful as our own.

We praise you, Oh God, for with you there is mercy. Blot out the sin of pride from among us and cause our hearts to be gladdened with your forgiveness. May you alone be exalted.
Amein.

INTRODUCTION

Forgive Me for My Jealousy

Jealousy is directly related to wounded pride and self-pity. We believe another has been given better looks, better skills and talents, greater opportunities, more affluence or a larger quantity of positive things in life and the list goes on. We compare ourselves to others, even if unconsciously, and believe we have been overlooked or somehow slighted.

In Judaism, jealousy is related to covetousness; desiring things that belong to others. We can envy a natural virtue within another's characters, desire someone they have in their lives or crave to own the goods they have acquired. In Genesis and again in Deuteronomy, we are given the command – do not covet. Our jealous desires can drive us to catch up with the next guy, to overtake him or even surpass him in ways that harm ourselves and others. They can cause us to plot, cheat and steal and worst of all – to kill.

The way to conquer jealousy is similar to wining over wounded pride; we must learn to be content with who we are, what we are and what we have. When we compare ourselves only with ourselves, we can work toward greater achievements based on our own performance. If we want a better job, we secure greater education and experience. If we wish to acquire a more pleasing appearance, we can engage a program of nutrition and exercise. If greater social abilities are what we seek, we can read books giving insight into personality types and align with more outgoing friends and colleagues. However, what happens when we cannot change certain aspects of our person, circumstances or background? We must accept.

Self-acceptance is a major theme throughout ancient and modern Judaism. Leviticus 19:18b says we are to love our neighbor as ourselves. First, we love ourselves. A jealous person has need of more self-love. To focus on the good fortunes of others, accepting them as the standard, is not loving of self or accepting of our own unique design. As with wounded pride, we are focused on our short-comings and what we do not have rather than our good points and what we possess. Also, as in the case of injured pride; we may reduce ourselves to a life of dissatisfaction concerning what God has chosen.

Jealousy tells us that an injustice has occurred in the way we were created; that somehow God was in error when He gave us a certain pair of ears, tone of voice, tone of skin, skill set, family or country of origin. There is no end to the variations among us. To compare, rather than accept, will beget a life of endless frustration and striving which robs of those positive qualities and things we possessed all along. A naturally cheerful person can become negative. One with superior intelligence can succumb to depression and lose the ability to focus and analyze.

The remedy for jealousy is to accept one's lot and be thankful for it. Judaism teaches that all is from God. The best job and the loss thereof; both are from Him. An imperfect smile and pleasant eyes, a grand home and a vehicle that breaks, excellent health and terminal illness – all are from Him. So, we recognize His work among us and are thankful for His governing hand; knowing all He does is filtered through His unending mercy. Jealousy covets. It compares. It is not thankful. It is touchy and irritable, complaining and striving, mean and base. We overcome jealousy with thankfulness for who and what God made us to be. We trust He has made no mistakes in all He has created and teach others the same, so they may be free from jealousy toward us.

PRAYER
Forgive Me for My Jealousy

Avinu Malkeinu, our Father and our King, forgive us for our sin of jealousy. Illuminate us with your glory and cause us to perceive your full, open and outstretched hand toward all. Help us to fix our gaze upon you; creator, giver and sustainer of all we are and will be. You alone have instilled within us the essence of life and sustenance of character. You alone have made us and not we ourselves. Fan within us the spark of hope and understanding to accept all you have given and withheld.

May we not covet the possessions, status or natural abilities of our neighbors, nor crave the goods, titles or powers within our societies and other peoples. May we nurture the love of self, the love of our brethren and love of others to whom we are not kin. Help us, Oh God, to look to you and be radiant as you give life to all, and sustain all and bestow blessing upon all according to your will and purposeful design. Cause us to rise in worship of your sovereign goodness and kingship over all and rid us of our jealousy.

INTRODUCTION

Forgive Me for My Inferiority

All around us we are bombarded by messages that tear down rather than build our feelings of personal worth. Visual media convinces that we fall short of the ideal appearance; we leave college, degree in hand, ready for the fight to obtain the best entry level position only to strive for promotion for the rest of our careers. Time after time we shy away from enacting our best ideas, from pursuing long awaited opportunities, from making needed changes in our circumstances or relationships – due to feelings of inferiority. We miss chances to express ourselves, to honestly communicate our needs and desires, to step forward to help others or to step back and let others take their places; all due to inferiority. Naturally, we fear failure, ridicule and embarrassment. This tendency stems from feelings of inadequacy when compared with others. Like pride and jealousy, inferiority tells us we don't measure up and can stifle the good things we are as it screams what we are not.

In Judaism, self-hatred springing from feelings of inferiority when compared to other peoples, was first recognized in the 1930's. It was seen as a social-psychological phenomenon in which individuals and groups within Judaism related all the maladies and misfortunes of their lives to being Jewish. The prejudices of others added to this social illness until the rebirth of the State of Israel in 1948. At that time, the forward attitude of most Jewish people aligned with self-acceptance as a viable and worthy people able to regroup, restructure and regain a place of pride and hope after the anti-Semitic oppression, death and destruction of the Nazi regime.

Inferiority has been an ancient struggle of the Jewish people and the Jewish individual. Whereas other populations of the world may face the same difficulties in milder degrees or in localized areas, the Jewish people have been deemed inferior or troublesome worldwide since the beginning of their existence. At times they have succumbed to the beliefs and ridicule of their opponents and at others stood together as one for self-dignity and respect.

Judaism teaches that each person has a positive and negative infusion of self-esteem which must be understood and personally corrected while on this earth. The positive is humility about one's value and importance and the negative is depressive inferiority which plummets the soul into fear and anxiety. In order to keep both inferiority and overweening pride at bay, the Jewish soul again looks to God. We possess a bit of His nature, but not too much. Therefore, pride over Him is certainly foolish just as is superiority above any of our fellows. On the other hand, having a bit of our Creator does place us above the animal kingdom and affords us to interact with the divine as a specialized creation. We are inferior to God, superior to animals and equal with each other. When all views are balanced we are at ease, productive and fulfilled. Inferiority alone accuses God of making a mistake while knitting us together, as King David explains, and superiority levels us with the absurd that would seek to overtake our Creator. Equality assures health.

PRAYER
Forgive Me for My Inferiority

Avinu Malkeinu, our Father and our King, forgive us for our inferiority. Remind us of our position in your creation, among the inhabitants of this world and our role in your sovereign plan. Help us to value our place as servants to you; our perfect, merciful and all-knowing Master and as emissaries to the world which you have created according to your will.

Forgive us for our lack of confidence, for struggles with fear, rejection and failure and for charging you with giving less than we deserve. Help us to recognize the good within us, the strength we can achieve and the success of which we are capable; as gifts from your hand. May we desist with self-criticism as much as negative self-pride. May we find our worth in you, in us as your people and our contribution to the welfare of humanity. When we fall prey to depression and self-deprecation cause us to cast off the bonds of gloom and receive with joy the assurance of your divine plan, purpose and mindfulness in our behalf.

Oh God, God of our forefather's, God of Abraham, Isaac and Jacob, enlighten us with your Torah. Turn your ear to our pleas for mercy and grant us pardon. Forgive us for our feelings of inferiority, self-doubt and anxious foreboding. Enlarge our hearts toward self-love, love of our brethren and goodwill toward all you have created. May we serve you with gladness of heart, confidence of mind and willingness of hands. Enlarge the place beneath our feet that we may stand on solid ground in fullness of your favor; steadied before our foes for the sake of your glory. Forgive us, Oh God, when we error toward inferiority. Strengthen us and we will be strong; forgive us and we will be forgiven; for the sake of your great name.
Amein

INTRODUCTION

Forgive Me for not being a Positive Person

Each new day brings a new opportunity to decide how each hour and each moment of that particular day will be lived and viewed. From the moment we open our eyes, and sit up to throw our feet over the edge of the bed, we are processing thoughts and setting a course before our feet touch the floor. If we are well rested and waking to a peaceful environment, with a meaningful day ahead, we may be propelled with a positive attitude. If we slept very little, awoke feeling lethargic and walked out the front door dreading the demands of the day, we may find ourselves dragging each foot toward the driveway.

Life is full of positive and negative, joy and sorrow, dread and delight. The same person who laughs in the morning may cry in the afternoon and the one that drenched their pillow with tears may have cause to rejoice in the morning. Nothing stays the same. The negative aspects of life do not stay forever just as the positive aspects do not linger beyond their time. All things pass, the good and the bad, but we remain. What matters most is the way in which we carry on.

In Judaism, we have many prayers that are recited at special and exacting times. It's the prayers that matter, not our attitude or connection to them. So why pray them if they do not emanate from the heart? The fact is they do emanate from the heart, the deeper self that acknowledges and accepts that all things are from God. However, our minds do not always agree since that is where our thinking, reasoning and dealing with each circumstance find their lodging place. Our minds think something is good, difficult or impossible. Our minds think something is easy, beautiful, workable or fair. The mind changes while the heart does not. The heart knows that things will resolve, that they'll work out as so many times before and that peace will return. The mind struggles with questions such as how will they work out, when, where and who will be involved. The mind asks why then wrestles with possible answers, many times becoming more confused than at the start. Why allow the heart to pray when the mind is not convinced? For the Jewish person, it is due to the constancy of God.

God is outside of time and space. He is not confined or restricted. He is all present, all knowing, all sufficient and all able. Because He is constant and reliable, because He is perfect in the constructing of our lives, we elevate ourselves above our thoughts to those things believed in the heart. Everything is from God and all will work perfectly, whether we understand or not.

Therefore, as we open our eyes in the morning we recite a prescribed prayer thanking God for returning our souls to us that we may live another day as He has allowed. It is during the hours of sleep when we are naturally closest to death, being unconscious and vulnerable, unaware and disconnected. When we open our eyes once more, we give thanks.

There are certain times of the year when another prayer is recited giving thanks for the present time or season. This is when we celebrate prescribed feasts and festivals and rejoice that the times have arrived. We credit God for creating us, sustaining us and bringing us to that season.
It doesn't matter if we arise with a headache, with a difficult meeting ahead or empty pockets when the mortgage is due; it doesn't matter if a festival rolls around when we are ill, have lost a loved

one or are too stressed to pause and celebrate. We give thanks. Thanks for each new day, each special time and prescribed season. If our Jewish ancestors could muster the courage and resolve to recite both prayers while facing the horrific conditions and uncertainties of concentration camps, we can certainly do the same in our relatively peaceful and non-threatened lives.

PRAYER
Forgive Me for not being a Positive Person

Avinu Malkeinu, our Father and our King, forgive us for not remaining a positive people. Have mercy upon us when we lament. Remember the struggles of our ancestors and those who in times of great sorrow poured out their tears to you. Forgive our feebleness and forgetfulness; cause us to recall your many compassions and goodness to us.

Though war rise up against us, though individual foes confront; calm us in your love and assure us with your hope. When we are tempted to turn aside and to complain as if orphaned and alone, remind us of your presence; still us with your peace.

May we be swifter to give thanks, quicker to praise and more diligent to ponder your kindness among us so that the voice of complaint is silenced and thoughts of despair vanquished. Forgive us for the negative thought and word. May we be a people that remembers your great care. May we recall all your benefits to us and your abundant pardon. Forgive us for when we do not remain positive and reposed.
Amein.

INTRODUCTION

Help Me Forgive my Enemies

It is said that one man's enemy is another man's friend. It is also said that man can be his own worst enemy. It is well known that partners in crime can become opponents before a judge and a husband and wife, once thrilled with the sight of one another, can end up sparring with accusations before a judge. It could be that we experienced our first encounter with an enemy on the school playground or perhaps even within our own homes earlier on. We are surrounded by enemies on varying levels and we ourselves are the enemies of others.

We read of the first enemies in the book of Genesis when Cain killed his brother Abel. They were not recorded as mutual enemies but one cultivated hatred of the other and rose up against him. From that time onward we can read of enemies large and small appearing and disappearing in the history of mankind. All we need do is turn on the TV or radio or open a news app on our cell phones and we are bombarded with the things enemies do to each other. When we sit before our computer screens, there it is again. Enemies are all around us; whether they are ours or someone else's.

This situation may seem impossible and give reason to barricade ourselves safely in our homes or to avoid unfamiliar, human contact as much as possible. However, it is also from other humans that we receive love. Friends and foes are ours to have.

Within Judaism, the subject of our enemies is a complicated one. As a point of reference, think of the noisy neighbor you'd like to move away. Think of the uncooperative coworker from which you'd like to distance yourself. Think of the person that cheated you out of something rightfully yours, the gang that sprayed graffiti upon your home, the person that harmed your child, the regime that murdered your entire family or the nation that would like to eliminate you and your people from the face of the earth. All of these scenarios represent some level of antagonism toward you or your loved ones. They speak of an offensive move against you and yours. So, how do we deal with the forgiveness of our enemies? We do good to them as far as it is possible; good deeds toward an enemy speaks of forgiveness without enlisting God's help to forgive. In Judaism, the prayer would most accurately ask for strength, courage and opportunity to do good to our enemies. However, we do not pray for such strength of mercy to all levels of our enemies; there are those of which we ask God to avenge in our behalf.

In the Torah, the first five books of the Jewish Bible or Tanakh, we are told to help our enemies as needed. King Solomon instructed against rejoicing when our enemy fails and not to be glad when he or she stumbles. Later in the book of Proverbs, Solomon says to feed our hungry enemy and if he is thirsty to give him a drink. So we attempt to discipline our evil inclination toward those who have harmed us by taking positive actions that benefit.

There are times when punishment is warranted toward those who have committed outstanding crimes. Again in the Torah, in the book of Deuteronomy, we read to leave such vengeance to

God; He will repay certain wrongs in our behalf. At other times we are instructed to fight for ourselves and to defend those who are under attack. Yet, on a day to day basis as one fellow deals with another who has in some way become an opponent, we ask for help to do good toward that person; then we do it.

PRAYER
Help Me Forgive my Enemies

Avinu Malkeinu, our Father and our King, help us do good to those who mistreat and use us. Imbue us with strength, courage and kindness to stretch forth our hands with deeds of righteousness toward all who offend. Cause us to rightly discern those to which we may extend a gesture of brotherhood and good will from those who would seek to destroy us. Cause our hearts to reach forward with understanding, compassion and assistance to those who would request of us by word or occasion of need.

Take vengeance, Oh Lord, on those of whom you would take vengeance. Pardon those which you would pardon. Sustain those which you would sustain. Help us meet each traveler upon the paths of life with charity and justice and to regard the welfare of the other as our worthy as our own.

Forgive us, Oh God, for withholding in anger, when it was in our power to return good for evil and mercy for injustice. Help our lips to refrain from rejoicing at the fall of our enemies and may we be silent at the vengeance of your hand. Elevate our souls toward regard for all men, grant respite from our foes and goodliness of response in the day of confrontation.
Amein.

INTRODUCTION

Help Me Forgive my Boss

For every place of employment and for everyone employed is someone who's in charge; who oversees, delegates, coaches and rewards, demands and scrutinizes, hires and fires. It matters not if he or she is referred to as manager, supervisor, team leader or captain…they are the boss. Anyone who has ever been hired knows they must please this boss, if possible, and to displease means write ups, counseling sessions, warning letters and possibly a long and final walk out to their cars. Bosses get to boss. Employees get to comply. To think that millions of people go to work each day and then again the next, is rather remarkable. People who are unrelated and otherwise disconnected unite for a specified number of hours each day and hold their positions for years on end. Some will retire with nice-sized pensions and others will go from job to job in search of a better work atmosphere, benefits and pay and nearly all will experience the sting of a boss's reprimand.

Many negative interactions with our bosses can be remedied by examining ourselves to see where personal improvement is needed. If we're in the habit of arriving late, coming ill prepared, missing deadlines or not following instructions, it is within our power to correct ourselves and avoid further confrontation. If we genuinely do not know or understand what is expected of us, we must speak up and get clarity so we may do our best. However, there are times when no matter how well we understand and perform our duties we will have a boss that is difficult and unfair. This is when our personal work ethic and faith must come to our aid. The strength to trudge into a work-place day after day when our supervisors are ill-tempered, ill-mannered or unclear with their desires, yet very clear with their insults, takes much self-control and resolve.

Why do we work? We need money. We need to satisfy our basic needs and those of our families. There are things we want to purchase, places we wish to visit, people we would like to see and entertain. We want to save for times ahead. We would like to do something we enjoy. We don't want to stay alone all day. The reasons to work are simple, yet they get lost when we face ongoing friction with those overseeing our lives for a good part of the day.

The primary way to endure is to keep our reasons for working clearly in view. We need to pay the mortgage and we want to take that week-end trip to the ocean. Next, we evaluate if a job change would be better, so we quietly look to improve our circumstances. Then we leave. To stay on the job in combat mode won't last and to stay while growing depressed or developing health problems will not benefit either. Therefore, unless our bosses are personally threatening with danger or harassing so that we may be abused – we must forgive.

However, as with any other enemy, Judaism doesn't directly teach to pray for help to forgive, but strength and courage to do well toward the one who antagonizes. In this way, we enact forgiveness rather than giving it mere mental ascent. The irritable boss is no exception. We look for ways to improve our performance and to assist our overseers for their personal good. This does not mean we neglect our own wellbeing or that of our families, but while we are on the job
we do our best to show acts of kindness toward our supervisors. Such actions not only possess the power to produce positive change in our bosses but also in us. Few people would reject an act of kindness. We can improve another's day which in turn improves our own.

PRAYER
Help Me to Forgive my Boss

Avinu Malkeinu, our Father and our King, strengthen us to do well toward those who employ us. May we regard their authority and comply with their reasonable, worthy and ethical requests. Empower us to understand and perform our duties well so we produce around us an atmosphere of personal peace which reflects to those within our influence. Give us wisdom and understanding to speak and enact according to the good of our fellow as well as our own.

When we face insult, help us to respond sincerely with respect. When we endure reprimand, may we listen and examine ourselves for the truth. When those is positions over us are unduly rude, unkind and demanding help us to answer with words and deeds befitting of kindness. Open our eyes to see the needs of our enemies so we may bestow upon them goodness and assistance in their time of want.

Strengthen us to do good to all and to repay with pleasantness the ills done to us in the workplace. May we be known to our overseers as diligent in work, knowledgeable of our positions, fair in our responses and patient with injustice. May prosperity come to us, to our coworkers and to each who manages; in our persons, in sustenance and in security of future.
Amein.

INTRODUCTION

Help Me Forgive You for not Answering My Prayers

When we think about prayer, we may think too much. We may slip from praying to meditation to just thinking and wishing. We may believe every thought that crosses our minds to be a sort of prayer. We may think every feeling of heart is a type of prayer. Imagine, although it's impossible; to see, hear and understand each whim of thought and word as if we were God. This is a difficult concept. To reduce the Almighty to words and ideas and to guess how the Creator of the universe receives and replies to prayers is beyond our finite reasoning and ability – yet we accuse Him of not hearing or answering.

To get a glimpse of the divine in our human understanding, we could think of a child beseeching a parent. The child asks. The parent may indulge the child's wishes, reply with resounding disapproval, tell the child to wait or remain quiet. The sound of "no" or foreboding silence can churn the stomach and produce tears. When we are the parent, these things are more easily understood. When we are the child, our feelings are roused. We may plead further with what we feel is even greater cause to obtain our wishes. We may cry, pout or accuse of injustice. We may stomp away sulking in solitude or destroy the things we do possess while longing for what we don't. We may walk away quietly, accepting the ruling of our parent and trusting their wisdom. Although our eyes may sting with tears and our hearts ache as if crushed, we understand that it is for our good.

In Judaism, we recognize God's sovereignty. We understand that all He does is perfect, holy, righteous, loving and just. It does not mean we understand what is perfect, holy, righteous, loving and just. It does not mean we discern each of those things in any given situation, but we acknowledge the presence of our God. He holds the answers to the things which perplex our human minds and confound our feeble hearts. We know He hears the prayers of His children, but we don't understand how He answers. What may seem a "no" may actually mean "wait." Sometimes, long after we've left off with a certain request, the desired end comes our way and we understand that timing was paramount and the wait warranted.

And so we pray. And we pray again. And we continue to pray. And we wait and long and become restless, but still we pray. In Judaism, we pray throughout the day. We start by giving thanks for being awakened, we pray ancient prayers that send us off into our day, we give thanks upon seeing a rainbow or a newborn child, or even someone who is of awkward appearance. We pray after our stomachs are satisfied, after we relieve ourselves, when we are ill, when we are in want. We close the day with the recitation of the Shema – Hear oh Israel, the Lord our God, the Lord is one… Jewish prayer is greatly about thanksgiving, and declaration of the personage of God and our relationship to Him. The matter of request is distant from these two primary purposes.

For the Jew, one of the darkest times of recent history was the horror of the Holocaust. For sure, many of us were praying. Some of us gave up. Some of us changed our prayers to angry accusations. Some of us wished there was no God! For if there were…why did we go to the gas chambers and ovens?

Many prayers went unanswered, as far as our understanding, yet we do not forgive God. We respond to Him. How do we respond to the One who created us, sustains us and brings us to such times and seasons? Is there need to forgive the God who is perfect, holy, righteous, loving and just? To do so would be a mere human exercise to relieve our weary selves since God, who does no wrong, is not at fault. Forgiveness deals directly with the fault of another. With God, no fault exists. So, we do not forgive Him but acknowledge His supremacy and our lack of understanding. We respond with continual thanksgiving for what we have and new requests for what we lack. We go to Him for greater strength, courage and peace.

PRAYER
Help Me to Forgive You for not Answering my Prayer

Avinu Malkeinu, our Father and our King, hear our cry for mercy. Give ear to our complaint. Who do we have but you? To whom can we turn and of whom can we inquire? You alone are God and to you alone we look. We wait for you. In the morning, we will beseech you. In the night we stretch forth our hands to you. We wait, longing for the sound of your deliverance.

Oh God, our God, hear us, answer us, do it for the sake of your great name. Do it for the sake of our ancestors. Do it for the sake of your beloved. Blot out our transgressions, dry our tears, uphold, strengthen and sustain. Cause us to hear the glad sound of your salvation. Bless your people with peace. Oh Israel, hope in God, for He will yet save.
Amein.

INTRODUCTION

Teach Me peace through Forgiveness

In the segment of Jewish prayer involving our enemies, we saw that forgiveness is an action not so much a word, feeling, thought or even a conversation. This type of forgiveness involves an offense committed by another toward us. It speaks of a positive response to a negative action taken against us by an enemy. In this section, we will look at forgiveness from the perspective of being the offender; for we have enemies and are the enemy.

The Torah tells us not to harbor ill toward or brother and not to take revenge. Our brothers are also to treat us in kind. They are to forgive us, just as we do them. In Judaism, we are taught that every Jew is responsible for his brother. This means we clear up all misunderstandings, assist wherever and whenever we can and promote the good of our people as a whole. If we have spoken words against our brother we must go to him and ask for forgiveness to clear up the matter and, as much as possible, with others that carried our words. If we cheated our brother, we are to repay and give above and beyond to heal his sadness. If we withheld information that may have benefitted our brother, we must go to him and provide all that we can for his good. The list is endless. When we have offended we must go to the brother and make things right. We are not to go to God about the matter until we have gone to our brother. This is the way of peace. To evade our brother, while seeking an audience with God, will not restore tranquility.

At the time of Yom Kippur, the yearly, day-long observation of fasting and repentance, we stand before God in congregations throughout the world. We enumerate a list of offenses we have committed against God and man. However, before we stand and touch our fists to our breasts while reciting our transgressions, we must have sought the forgiveness of our brethren.

There was once an elderly man, who stood up during a service just before Yom Kippur and asked the entire congregation to forgive him for any offenses he may have committed toward any one of them. He then asked for forgiveness for anything he should have done in their behalf's but did not. None could deny this sincere and humble man standing before dozens of gazing eyes. And so it should be whenever we feel the pangs of guilt and remorse toward our brethren. We should not wait for the weeks before the biblical and national day of repentance; but initiate forgiveness year round. Keeping short accounts of our mistakes will do the best good to our fellow and for ourselves. We swallow our pride and make things right.

There is a definite peace when we have cleared all things with those around us; it sets the stage for setting things right with God. We can approach Him with the assurance that since we have done our prerequisite homework, we can ask His forgiveness and be pardoned on the greater level. So, the way of peace remains…we ask our brother for forgiveness, we ask God for forgiveness and then we are restored to a state of rest and relaxation of conscious.

This same path of peace can be utilized when dealing with the non-Jew. Wherever we have offended we must attempt to reconcile for the good of humanity. However, when dealing with overt actions of others against us, our forgiveness may not seem as clear. When we are not asked to forgive, and the antagonism is ongoing, we do our best to perform deeds of goodness whether or not dialogue will ever transpire.

Forgiveness is a circle. It is always necessary, always healing and always the right thing to do. The more we forgive others the more they, and we ourselves, are impacted for the good.

PRAYER
Teach Me Peace through Forgiveness

Avinu Malkeinu, our Father and our King, help us to walk in the path of forgiveness toward our brothers and all who ask of us. May we be swift to approach all we have offended and be diligent to restore the brokenness of others as you direct and enable. May we consider the peace of our brother as dear as our own and submit ourselves to reconciliation. May we run to establish understanding and pardon, and to abase ourselves before our fellow regarding his wholeness greater than our shame, pride or embarrassment.

Help us, Oh God, to perceive our faults, to be responsible and restore for the good of all. Reinstate us for peace along with all those who seek peace. And may peace and tranquility come to all men according to your great purpose. Forgive us and we will be forgiven. Restore us and we will be restored. Settle us and we will be at peace.
Amein.

INTRODUCTION

Forgive Me for not Feeling Supported

The writings of King David, found in the Psalms, are among the most loved and referred to portions of Jewish text. His candid and heart-felt expressions have given voice to worshippers of many faiths as they sing, recite and mournfully pray the words he penned for the God of Israel. This great king poured forth his complaints, fears, anger and sorrow as well as his joys, blessings, praises and victories. He was raw and real with his feelings and gives us courage to be the same. O God, help me for not feeling supported. David was the master of such sentiments.

The ways in which we feel alone are the same today as they were for our predecessors. We can feel void of help, comfort, love, attention, companionship and even void of God. We are frail in our understanding and prone to fears of many kinds. We desire to be surrounded with love and camaraderie, and in times of great testing we are acutely aware of that need. Where did everyone go? Why aren't they here for me and why aren't they helping? Does anyone care?

King David spoke of friends that were here today and gone tomorrow. Friends he had supported in their weakest states and most desperate moments vanished when he was troubled. He cried out to God with many tears when friends turned cold, were careless or became enemies. However, there were also times the king felt deserted by God. When that happened, he sought the Almighty and was recorded as being a man after God's own heart.

It may seem odd to pursue the Creator but in Judaism, that's exactly what we do. He does not run away nor purposely ignore, such as happens when one person disconnects from another, He merely waits for us to approach. He is not far in location nor distant in character. He desires our closeness and is ready to be apprehended. In David's anguish of soul, he says many things that are absurd; things which may seem irreverent, but the God of Israel is patient, kind and abounding in love toward all He has made.

David accuses God of having turned away, of not listening, not seeing and not responding to his cries for help. He recounts his miseries, describing each one in detail, then ultimately concludes with the same, enduring truth – God is there, He has heard, He does see and He will hasten to support. With this assurance, David rises to trust again. However, he will be found in the throes of lament another time and then another, and like we, he cries out, the trial passes and blue skies return. Is it any surprise, given the gut-level honesty of David, that his words are world-renown for both praise and complaint?

When we feel unsupported, we can pull away from loved ones who do support in the ways they are able, but our inner turmoil tricks us into believing we are alone. At times, there is nothing that can be done but to wait things out. And of course, there are instances when others are too busy, distracted or miss chances to be by our sides; just as we have failed to be available for them. Ultimately, just as David said, our help comes from God. He may prompt others to assist and succor, but even the best of intentions in the hearts of our friends and family come not from themselves but the spark of the divine within.

PRAYER
Forgive Me for not Feeling Supported

Avinu Malkeinu, our Father and our King, forgive us when we feel abandoned. When friends and family cannot be found and troubles mount, may we come before you. When it seems you have turned away and our cries are turned back upon us, help us remain steadfast in our prayers before your throne. Forgive us when we cry as orphans, when we accuse of estrangement or contemplate with scorn. May our eyes ever be toward you and our supplications rise in confidence.

O God, God of our forefathers, God of Abraham, Isaac and Jacob hear us. As you aided our fathers, be our aid and support. As you heard them in the deserts, wastelands and encampments, hear our pleas for mercy. Cause us to remember your many kindnesses to your people and to wait for you with gladness, for with you is sure salvation.

Our Eternal King, forgive us when we speak from our frailties. Remember the dust from which you have wrought us and take pity. Though we be dejected and thoughts of abandonment surround, show your tender mercies. Aid us with your loving-kindness, secure us with your might. May we look to you and rejoice. May our hearts remember your multiplied blessings upon us and give you thanks. Forgive us, O God, when we feel unsupported.
Amein.

INTRODUCTION

Forgive Me for not Taking Enough Time for Myself

In our fast-paced world of pressures to perform, decisions to make, people to care for and ever-multiplying facets of the business of life, we can forget our first business – that of self-care. Who can perform well when they are not rested and well-nourished? Who can make wise and sensible decisions if they are not alert? Who can care for the needs of others when they have not learned to care for their own? Who can rise to the demands of everyday life, with all its preplanned ventures and spontaneities, without having taken the time for strengthening both inside and out?

We may rush through each day as a freight train down-hill, with speed and momentum that cannot stop. As night falls, and mind and body beg for relaxation, we may push further with activity until the hours for sleep are but few and we awake to the screaming sound of the alarm. We drag from our homes and again it's all down-hill; fast and furiously. However, just ahead is something that will grind to a halt; may it not be serious illness, loss of relationship or mental breakdown.

Taking time for ourselves is something we must do. Just as we clean the house, pay the bills, attend meetings and drive the car. We just do it. Just as we plan to go here and there and accomplish this and that and see this loved one and this business person; we take care of ourselves with the same certainty. We must make it happen just as we do all the other things that constitute life.

In Judaism, we read that we must not kill. At face value, this seems not to take the physical life of another human being. However, it means much more. If we do not care for our bodies, minds and souls we are in fact enacting a slow suicide, which Judaism also forbids. Neither do we deprive another of wellbeing in these same areas. If we neglect ourselves, that is not to show love to our own person, we cannot love and care for others for their highest good.

Observant Jewish life focuses on prayer, good health, proper relationships, education, charity and rest.
The seventh day of our week, the Sabbath, is devoted to our rejuvenation with a focus on prayer services, celebratory foods, casual visits with friends, leisurely walks and afternoon naps. There is no business allowed; no shopping, no monetary transactions, no mowing of lawns, no washing of cars, no vacuuming, no dishes, no travel and nothing of anything else that resembles the work-week. We separate the common from the sacred, work from rest, Sabbath from the other six days.

This is not to say that we abuse ourselves throughout the week in order to fall into our easy chairs for a mere twenty-four-hour respite. Our weekly prayers focus on thanksgiving for the mundane and the spectacular and remind us to take care of ourselves and our brothers. Our rabbis, our religious school teachers and our camp counselors also direct toward the nurturing of body, mind and soul. For those of us still blessed with the presence of our grandmothers, another source of reminders is to be had.

Contemporary medicine and mental health professionals agree that to take time for oneself and to clear away a space for retreat provides greater quality of life and longevity. The two-week vacation crammed between the other fifty-two weeks of frenzy is not sustaining. We must learn to quiet ourselves daily, to eat nutrition-rich foods, to exercise more, to sleep longer and to maintain peace within ourselves and well as in our outer worlds, as much as possible. When we have neglected to maintain or to remediate the care of self we must resolve to improve and if needed enlist the help of others. At times, damage has been done and to recover our wholeness is difficult if not impossible. We must take all these things to our creator; the One who knows us best, and ask for His merciful and healing hand upon us.

PRAYER
Forgive Me for not Taking Enough Time for Myself

Avinu Malkeinu, our Father and our King, forgive us for our neglect of self. You who has created and sustained us, you alone, O God, know of our comings and goings, our works, our deeds and our times of rest. You who has given us times and seasons of gladness and joy, refrainment of work and toil and blessings of health, sleep and comfort; forgive us when treat with disrespect our beings which you have created.

Refresh our resolve to observe your Sabbaths, infuse us with determination to treat kindly our bodies, minds and souls in accordance with your commands. Provide for us other times of respite and repose, cessation of turmoil and grief, seasons of ease and restoration. Be patient with our failed attempts and spur us on to more fervent efforts. Open our minds to understand what is good, perfect, right and just as we nurture ourselves and those within our care. Restore our health and soundness, O God, according to your bountiful mercies.
Amein.

INTRODUCTION

Forgive Me for not Spending Quality Time with my Pets

In Proverbs 12:10 King Solomon writes, "A righteous man cares for the needs of his animal." Of course, pet owners and those who dislike animals in the living space of humans, will disagree as to what are the needs of an animal. However, if we have pets, we should have the best intentions for them in every way. We feed, water and maintain their health as minimal, but they also, as creations of God, deserve love and attention. Most of us have witnessed a dog leashed outside in all kinds of weather, who gets little more than scraps tossed his way at unpredictable times. We've seen the stray cats and unwanted kittens and heard stories of big-game hunters wanting nothing more than to mount trophies upon their walls.

In recent years human-interest groups have led way to animal interest groups and now the neglected, abused and homeless among our furry friends can be adopted into loving homes just as newborn babies and foster children. I don't many who can resist the warm, brown eyes of a puppy or the sweet face and charming antics of a kitten, but our care must go beyond those first, endearing months in the lives of our pets. Just as our children grow and change and we all face the process of aging, so it is with our pets.

King Solomon connected righteousness with the way a man cares for his animals. If we read the passage in the converse, we would see that a wicked man does not care for the needs of his animal. Perhaps this same man does not care for the needs of family either, but whatever the case, it is right and praise-worthy to make sure everyone and everything thing in our homes are there because they are wanted; and they know it.

Forgive us for not spending quality time with our pets. First, I believe we should know what our particular pet needs. Arming ourselves with knowledge is an easy task with much information on the internet and willing breeders, 4-H club members and pet ownership groups ready to share their expertise. Today's veterinarians are more interested in an animal's psyche than in earlier years and dog groomers, spas, pet play groups and canine, vacation kennels provide hands-on experience with the latest techniques in animal wellness. We can firmly conclude that spending quality time with our pets is another one of those things we must – just do. We must develop the habit. The information, the toys, the parks and the pet-gear are at our disposal. We must spring to action.

In the Jewish household many dogs and cats speak Hebrew. That is, the American Jew, in various attempts to keep a strong connection with Israel and the rebirth of the Hebrew language, have opted to name and train their pets in our ancient tongue. Most pets are regarded as family members and receive what may be seen as excessive pampering. However, who else do our animal, loved ones have, if not us? So, we tend to them as dearly as we would ourselves and realize the job is indeed ours with no occasion for laziness or excuse. When we have been lax, it is good to refer to our ancient Jewish text, the Tanakh, for a reminder concerning the acts of righteousness and God's injunction to mankind concerning animal welfare. God gave us the command to subdue the members of the animal kingdom and to care for them. Since we have been put in charge, we should endeavor to be kindly and trusted guardians.

PRAYER
Forgive Me for not Spending Quality Time with my Pets

Avinu Malkeinu, our Father and our King, thank you for the presence of animals you have created and for our pets which you have allowed into our lives. Help us to include among our acts of righteousness fair and goodly treatment of each one. Cause us to remember your command to subdue, in the sense of tending and providing loving oversight for the creatures you have made. Give us wisdom to discern their needs and may we recognize the insights we may gain from them concerning your kingdom of animals.

When we fail to tend properly or neglect to shower with love and consideration, please forgive our neglect and help us to cultivate a more urgent sense of responsibility. Help us to train our children toward the same and teach them through the companionship and trust we are given through our pets.

Blessed are you, King of the universe, who has filled the earth with life and given to us the responsibility of life, both of mankind and of animals. Forgive us when we prove to be unfaithful stewards of your creation.
Amein.

INTRODUCTION

Forgive Me for not Spending Quality Time with my Children

Of all the things we cherish in this life, our children out-rank them all. They bring the quickest laughter and tears, warm our hearts, cause our chests to swell with pride and dash us to the depths of despair. Most parents remember well that moment when they held their first, little bundle in their arms and their lives changed in an instant.

New moms may feel a sense of accomplishment like never before. There snuggled against their breasts, is a tiny he or she, warm, soft, wet, pink, blue and bewildered. And she loves that one profoundly. She's ready to figure out motherhood; ready to take her place in all the mommy circles and play groups and ready to recount her personal, birthing story with the other valiant women of the world. She knows she has done something heroic, but more than that, she is overtaken with profound attachment to this one breathing gently against her skin.

Dads may feel a since of the incredible as they watch their helpless, little guy or gal enter the world through the great effort, dedication and sacrifice of the woman they love. They may feel a load of responsibility like never before and wonder if they're up to the task. This crumpled, helpless and dependent creature is counting on them. It's time to daddy-up and embrace the role of protector, defender, provider, instructor and perhaps change a diaper for the first time in his life. And though he may not understand it all at that moment, they are now three, not two.

And then there's the baby gear and gadgets! How can such a small, non-mobile and sleep-oriented newborn need so much stuff? But we get it all, from combs and brushes to front packs to designer car seats. We buy more clothes than our sweet one can wear and if there's a safety device to ensure his or her lifespan to a hundred years – we'll purchase and install it! We love our babies. We love our toddlers and pre-schoolers, our pouting second graders, budding sixth graders, our middle school sport champs, our high-school art students and finally as we watch them walk the stage for graduations of all types and diplomas or degrees of all kinds, we feel we have loved that wrinkled, little mess into a secure future of their own. But we don't stop there. We can still be awoken at midnight and jump into the car to aid our adult children, perhaps with their own children or just because on that first day of their lives we knew they were ours forever; including whatever that would bring. Parents are parents for life.

Since we love our children so, how is it we can neglect to spend quality time with them? We may have no good answer. We may also have dozens of good reasons that fluctuate with time and circumstance. In Judaism, children are viewed as a gift from God. In fact, we are commanded to be fruitful and multiple and so we procreate. How wonderful when a followed command yields such life-long blessing. As a people, Jews are concerned with parenting issues such as ethnic identity and connection, education and the continuance of our generations – more babies. However, like most populations today, we have fewer children than days gone by and our lives are busy about communal and world affairs.

Time with our children can mean saying "no" to things we otherwise enjoy. We may need to get better at planning ahead, set limits on social activities and turn down extra, work hours. We may need to be more present in mind and attentiveness. A parent can be home physically, yet nowhere near in thought and engagement. God help us to show our children the love we have, so they must not assume its existence!

PRAYER
Forgive Me for not Spending Quality Time with my Children

Avinu Malkeinu, our Father and our King, thank you for the gift of our children. Thank you for entrusting us with their lives and supporting us as we nurture them into adulthood. Strengthen us to guide them in wisdom, discernment and understanding. Forgive us, O God, when we fail to be available as parents. Prompt us toward meaningful conversation and activity with our children and their children. Inspire us to teach them your Torah, that they may live a life of fruitfulness, satisfaction and good deeds. Help us model before them your will and your ways and instill in them a goodly heritage with love for your name.

Help us, Oh God, to see our failings with our children. Open our understanding to perceive the needs of each one and empower us to meet them according to your design. Where we have been negligent, allow us to reinstate and rekindle. Protect, lead, defend and provide for our children and grant to them health, wisdom and strength for continuance and longevity. Forgive us when we turn aside to other things, may we return to you and to our children for goodwill, preservation and posterity.
Amein.

INTRODUCTION

Forgive Me for My Lack of Faith

Faith can be described as something we believe without any proof of its validity or existence, or an allegiance to something or someone with which we choose to identify. It can also mean something more akin to hope, I have faith that the sun will rise tomorrow; I hope it will. It will. I have faith that it will.

Faith can be directly connected with a belief in God, many gods or a religion. In Judaism, faith is not so much of a belief or hope but an awareness of God; the Creator of the universe. We are aware of Him. That awareness causes us to pursue Him and the way of pursuit is prayer. We pray because we are aware of God and to refrain from prayer damages that awareness. He is here, there and everywhere, but we must pause to be aware, to acknowledge Him.

Throughout the Tanakh, we see prayer taking many forms. Our ancestors prayed for the mundane and the fantastic. Through prayer, babies were conceived, people were fed, water was found, wisdom was given, the sun stood still, the dead were resuscitated and years were added to a king's life. Through prayer, God was praised, men abased, solace was found and weeping ended. Prayer comprises worship, thanksgiving and complaint and in the case of King David – multilevel dialogue and song. Prayer emanates from our awareness of someone to pray to. Faith is awareness of our God. We lose faith, or awareness, when our lives are clouded by circumstances; whether good or bad.

A man of excellent health, prominent social status, soundness of character and ample wealth can lose awareness of the Almighty. He may see no need to stop and consider his God; life is good and faith is for those who are in need. A beggar, sitting on the corner in hopes of some act of charity, may also lose awareness. Both the affluent and the impoverished can lack faith; one is pleased with life and needs no upward focus, the other is burdened with life and believes such focus is futile; if he thinks beyond his dire needs at all. Most of us lie someplace between these two fellows. Life is up and down then steady and perhaps even boring, then busy and exciting and cycling back through all of the above. Our awareness waxes and wanes.

In Jewish tradition, we pray at least one hundred prayers each day. This is to maintain focus on God and His presence. One hundred prayers may seem impossible, but considering that many are prayed in conjunction with others or in the case of the Amidah, in a group of nineteen which are prayed three times per day by observant Jews, it isn't difficult to reach the goal. Although Jewish prayers are written down and recited repetitiously, they serve the purpose of keeping us aligned with faith, or awareness, when we have little energy or creativity to compose our own. However, as one rabbi put it, "A woman's prayers are best uttered over the dish water in her own words."

Jewish men meet three times each day in the synagogue to pray. Woman are welcome to join in and in the more liberal branches of Judaism, woman make their own minyan, or group of ten, needed to recite certain prayers and to remove the Torah from its ark or cabinet. In the Jewish heart and soul, a connection to God is primary, necessary and desired. To lose our awareness of Him is to lose faith, and in essence to lose ourselves, because He is why we are here in the first place. Without God's call to Abraham, we would not exist. Without His miraculous, protective and sustaining power, we would have ceased to be a people. And so, our faith, our awareness of Him, lives on.

PRAYER
Forgive Me for My Lack of Faith

Avinu Malkeinu, our Father and our King, forgive us for our lack of faith and awareness of your great name. Help us to recall your ways and your paths given to us of old. May we see you in the pages of your Torah. May we be mindful of your hand in our behalf throughout the writings of our ancestors and the prophets which spoke your words.

May we keep before us the evidence of your might among us, even as we ponder the miracle of Israel, our homeland. Help us, O God, to kindle the spark within, to seek after you and proclaim your name. May all come to an awareness of your fatherhood and kingship and place their hope in you.

O God of Israel, awake us from our slumber and cause us to acknowledge you. Forgive us when we lose faith and turn aside to things which usurp your rightful place. Let not depression, not gloom rule over us. Let not wealth, nor status distract us. May we wake to your presence and be illuminated by your glory as we seek your face.
Amein.

INTRODUCTION

Forgive Me for not Loving my Spouse Sometimes

Love is something we all need and at times do not wish to give. If we're tired and stressed, we may not be aware we are withholding our usual expressions of love or have replaced them with irritable words or behaviors. Of course, the one who is nearest to us will feel the brunt of our lack of love and affection; this is usually our spouses. Is it that we genuinely stopped loving or is love on hold, so to speak, waiting to be picked up again?

The things that place our love on hold are innumerable. They can be as simple as a frustrating day at work or with the kids or deep seated anger and strife with the power to tear the two apart. Simple breaks in our love can we remedied with greater care to emotional detail and follow through. We recognize our momentary coldness and quickly warm back up with a kind word or deed toward the one we hold dear. However, lack of love on a deeper level requires a careful examination, and perhaps third-party intervention, to restore husband and wife to a place of wholeness. Whichever the case may be, walking in love with the one we have pledged our lives to, is worthy of our highest concentration and efforts.

The Talmud says if women treat their husbands as kings, they will in turn be treated as queens. That may seem like a heavy responsibility and it may not always work, but if women give it their best, sincere and selfless effort it would be found out if it is to work or not. The Jewish husband is to ensure that his wife has everything that will cause her to feel lovely and is instructed to warmly give her the time and romance she needs. Imagine if both husband and wife initiated their own loving efforts toward one another based on nothing but their own resolve.

What is loving to one couple may not be to another. When we feel "out of love" for the moment, we would do well to remember one of the many connectors that bring our particular relationship back into function. If, as a couple, we enjoy chocolate milkshakes, then we need to go get one. If we love to walk the dog together, we need to go get the leash. If we need to watch that old movie for the twelfth time or cook spaghetti together or read a book out loud and discuss it or even go buy one or the other a new pair of gym shoes, we need to reconnect.

It can be helpful to have a list of loving actions each enjoys, tucked away for the rainy-days of a marriage. When we haven't been our best selves toward our spouses, we can consult with the list and chose an action to get us back on track in heart and action. Another tool is to change our thoughts. It is good to remember all the wonderful things our spouses are in character and the good they do toward us and our children or extended family. Gratitude goes a long way in reinstating the warmth in marriage as does humility.

In Judaism, humility is a desirable trait for all individuals and in all relationships. The Torah teaches humility toward God and man, with reverence toward God and sincere acts of care and concern for our neighbor. When we keep in mind what is desirable to ourselves, we can more easily do the same for our loved ones, especially our spouses.

PRAYER
Forgive Me for not Loving my Spouse Sometimes

Avinu Malkeinu, our Father and our King, forgive us for our lack of love. When we are tired and burdened, stressed and distracted or short on patience; help us to set aside our difficulties to focus our deeper selves on the one we love the most. When we are busy, help us to slow to a more considerate pace, when we entertain unloving thoughts toward our spouses, help us to replace them with gratitude toward who they are and for what they have done. When we have argued or taken unkind action, help us to make amends and seek full reconciliation with all humility.

Oh God, who has sanctified the union of husband and wife and has blessed with children, companionship and singleness of purpose toward you, help us to ever walk in unity above the matters of life and those things which desire to separate. Cause our hearts to entreat of one another and to hear the kindly answers of love and devotion. Help us to give freely and cheerfully and to lay aside annoyance and spite. Forgive us, O God, when we are unloving toward our spouses. Rekindled again our dispositions toward each other and renew us for longevity and prosperity. Amein.

INTRODUCTION

Forgive Me for Doubting Your Love for Me

Doubting God's love is easy, at first glance, but very difficult upon closer examination. The God of the universe, the Creator of all mankind and everything that exists, has surrounded us with infinite reminders of His wondrous love. The sun rises to give us warmth and the promise of a new day. It sets to give us beauty and repose and a time for rest and rejuvenation. Everywhere we look is God's hand of love and care. It is seen throughout nature, heard in the notes of a song and felt in the closeness of relationships. His love heals, encourages, exhorts and sustains. It can go unnoticed because it is so full, so free and so constant; like the air we breathe.

Imagine the feeling of having no oxygen. If God had indeed removed His love from us, we would know it in an instant and feel it beyond all doubt. However, we can subtly slip into questioning when in actuality He hasn't removed Himself at all. If He had, we would know for sure; He will not remove Himself.

In Judaism, we realize that God cannot and will not remove Himself from us. He is for us and toward us. A bit of Himself is in each one of us. He will not deny Himself. His compassions to us are new every morning. His faithfulness is great. And so, it is not He who refrains from loving, nor Him that injects the thought that He has ceased to care. It is within us that such notions are derived and find occasion to flourish. Yet, He is patient with our frailties.

A leisurely walk in the woods may help us remember He is near, listening, caring and loving. We take in the sights, sounds, smells and textures of His creation. The business of our normal affairs begins to fade away and although we may be unmindful, a cleansing has begun. We may find ourselves talking out loud as if to the wind, but He is near. We may purposefully direct a prayer to the heavens. We may cry out to Him or perhaps feel the need to scream. His presence abounds and He desires that we come away to find Him. He promises He will be found when we seek Him with all our hearts.

When in doubt of His infinite love, we may find comfort and reassurance within the pages of the Psalms. To repeat the words of King David, the man after God's own heart, is to join with the voices of millions throughout the ages wishing to find solace in the presence of the Almighty. Forgive us, O God, when we
doubt your love. Of course, He forgives; it's a sign that He does in fact love us, has not gone away and is not busy with other things. He is love and He is always present in His love for us.

PRAYER
Forgive Me for Doubting your Love for Me

Avinu Malkeinu, our Father and our King, forgive our many doubts. You are not a God who can be compared to mortal man. You are not changeable, nor undecided. You do not turn away from the work of your hands. Forgive us when we doubt your love. Forgive us when we dwell in sorrow as if you are not with us and when we complain as if your love is not enough. From ancient times, you have been our God and gently you have carried us.

As a father has compassion on his children, you have pitied us. As a mother cannot deny her nursing child, you have not turned us aside. Call us to remember your great care, your many kindnesses and your resplendent acts among us. Forgive, O God, when we forget. When we forget how you carried us out of Egypt where we bowed beneath the slave-driver's whip. Cause us to remember how you led us forth from Babylon and gave us favor so that our Holy Temple was restored. Illuminate our minds to consider your deliverance of old and your outstretched arm which delivers still. In love you called us from among the nations. In love you have sustained us to this day. In love you promise our tomorrows as your holy prophets have declared.

O God, Our God, forgive our accusations and bolster our hearts to ponder your love for us, our children and our children's children, yet unborn. You, who are good to all and loving to all, bear with us in your love and hasten the days of your Messiah. We wait for you. We wait for your salvation. Do good to your people Israel, do it for the sake of your great name. Do it for the sake of your unfailing love. Blot out our transgressions and secure us in your love.
Amein.

INTRODUCTION

Forgive Me for Harboring Hate for Those that Insult Me

It's easier to remember an insult than a compliment. The same person can praise us for an accomplishment then insult our handling of another situation and the insult sticks. It has been said that for every negative entry into our memory banks, it takes four positive ones to eliminate it. If that's the case, will we ever erase the negative?

We live in a world where people speak loosely. We use the word *love* to describe anything from our favorite flavor of ice cream to our relationship with our spouses. We use *hate* from our dislike of the neighbor's dog on our front lawns to our sentiments toward the criminal involved in a drive-by shooting. Our words lose meaning when used at random, except when they are directed in an insult.

If we said an apple is rotten, few would be offended. If we said the world is rotten, some may rebuke and interject their views concerning the beauty and goodwill they have experienced. However, if we tell a person *they* have a rotten attitude…that word suddenly invokes great feelings in the hearer. If we compliment the same person repeatedly for the rest of the week and enjoy their company for months going forward, chances are they will remember the time we spoke ill of their attitude. Likewise, the piercing words directed at us will linger.

The old saying, "Sticks and stones may break my bones but words will never hurt me" is a lie. In the book of Proverbs, found in the Tanakh, we read that life and death are in the power of the tongue. Also, rash statements are like the thrust of a sword and a whisperer separates close friends. Words go deep and can kill the soul and crush spirit. A child who has been verbally abused will emerge into adulthood with a brokenness that will in turn bring harm to others. A person who is careless with their words then claims to be jesting, is not well-liked and the one who engages in sarcasm, to insult another, is regarded as cruel.

However, words can heal. Proverbs says the tongue of the wise brings healing and a gentle tongue is a tree of life; it nourishes. And an often repeated verse speaks of words that are fitting; they are like apples of gold in settings of silver. They are lovely, refined, beautiful and fit. They are compatible with goodliness.

How do we respond when insulted? The knee-jerk reaction is to revile back or defend ourselves. If we are more passive, we may allow the offender to spew his or her words upon us while we remain silent or break to tears. We may quickly walk away. No matter how we react or respond, we will all ponder the incident later and that's when our brooding may get the best of us. If we have exercised the super-human discipline of silence when the incident took place, we can deal quietly with ourselves without regret for words or actions of our own. When the necessary work is within, we have a much greater chance of recovery. However, in the case of a child or adult exposed to ongoing barrage, an advocate is needed. When insults are few or otherwise within the scope of an average existence, although they are painful, we must do our best to move on through forgiveness and keeping our thoughts to other matters.

PRAYER
Forgive Me for Harboring Hate for those who Insult Me

Avinu Malkeinu, our Father and our King, forgive us for harboring hatred toward those who insult us. When words have risen up against us from our brethren, help us to forebear and forgive. When an enemy comes against us with slander or malicious speech, help us to hold our peace. When our minds recall the sting, help us to forgive. When we are tempted to hate whether in mind, word or deed, help us to refrain.

O God, our God, you see all and take to heart when we have been despised and ill-treated. You know each piercing of heart and injury to the soul. May we also guard our tongues and may our words be not the cause of pain to our brethren. As for our enemies, watch over and defend us, may we be known for peace, even as you give us peace. May we bridle our tongues; secure in your governance and protection.

Help us O God, to forgive in the day of insult, to do good toward all men and return our souls to rest, unfettered by cords of hate or malice. May all who speak ill be silent and may all who rise up take note and desist. O God of Jacob, be our stay, our ready defense and the source of all comfort. O Israel, trust in God and you shall not be moved nor forsaken.
Amein.

INTRODUCTION

Forgive Me for Believing You will not Heal my Soul

How does God heal the soul? In Judaism, we see two components working together to render healing. The body and the soul are so entwined that one cannot be healthy and the other lame. Most medical practitioners agree that illness in the body is closely related to illness of soul and treating both yields the best result. Cancer patients have experimented with meditation and other relaxation techniques to calm and restore all facets of health through purposeful exercises which balance hormones and provide nourishment to all body systems. The holistic approach to diseases of all kinds now incorporates the mind, or the mental and emotional state, as part of the fundamentals of healing.

Healing takes work. It requires mental and physical energy and a will to achieve harmony within ourselves. It is rarely completed in a day and once achieved we cannot return to our previous ways and expect to remain sound. For the Jew, pray and community involvement provide fertile ground for improvement. Prayer connects to God and community participation to those who help navigate the path. During times of deep pain, loss, stress and illness some of most formidable allies can be found and kept for a lifetime.

When we think of God as healer of body or soul we recognize we're going to the best. The One who has created and fashioned each individual certainly knows the ways to heal and restore His creation. Throughout the Tanakh, especially in the Psalms, we see the heart-wrenching details of the struggles of King David. He lays himself bear before God and laments of his woes. Some are physical, some emotional and others of social origin, but he is quick to run to the One who knows his every painful thought.

The older we get the more we are keenly aware that life will remain how it is; meaning we will see good and bad in perpetuity and if keeping a score card, there will most likely be more to the negative as we age and face challenges. We can determine to be better rather than bitter until we face the next assault and find ourselves down in the depths once more. Will healing ever come?

Judaism teaches that the toils of this life will cease and we'll be welcomed into heaven, after God has judged our deeds and motives. Before we reach our eternal destination, we may spend time in Sheol. This is where we are cleansed of sins not confessed in this earthly life then we take our place in heaven. True healing, lasting and complete, is only accomplished at this stage. Healing of soul before then is not expected, but sustaining of soul is. When we feel that God will not heal our inner person we must remind ourselves that He will at the appointed time. Until then, we look to Him with eyes of hope for each new day believing He is as near as our breath, ready to uplift and encourage. He is our Father and He will heal.

PRAYER
Forgive Me for Believing you will not Heal My Soul

Avinu Malkeinu, our Father and our King, hear our cries to you. From the depths of anguish, we have accused you and counted you among those who have no concern. Forgive us for our disbelief; for our hearts that turn away as if you are not among us. From our beginning, you have regarded us. You have heard our pleas and opened your hands to us. You are not a God who forgets. You do not forsake your people.

Forgive our sorrow and forlorn. Forgive our despondency. Lift our heads to gaze upon you and to praise your wondrous acts of mercy. For you alone have called and secured us. You alone have led us and sustained. We look to you. When the darkness overtakes us, we cry to you. From the depths you hear us and we are lifted out. You set our feet in a goodly place and steady our ankles, so we do not slip. You alone stand us aright and in you we place our hope.

May the onlookers see and declare your glory. May all who see us know you are faithful. You will restore. You will heal. You will satisfy our souls with your goodness and heal the broken places. You will take us up and bring us to yourself. You will touch the broken chords and renew our song before you. You will dry each tear and cause the legs, once crippled, to dance before you.

O God, forgive us. With perfect faith we are assured of your love and might. With perfect faith we look to you. Restore us and heal us according to your loving kindness.
Amein.

INTRODUCTION

Forgive Me for not Believing in You

The subject of belief in God is the biggest, determining factor is a person's life. It sets the course for all other beliefs and dictates a person's actions and path of life. If we do not believe in our Creator, then we have no origin of worth. If we do not believe in a loving, heavenly Father, we have no place of destiny. To be born, live and die with nothing more than our fleshly skin, void of enduring spirit; is to be faced with the question, "Is this all there is?" If answered in the affirmative; what a sad lot for mankind.

Throughout Jewish history, our people have struggled with God. In fact, in the Hebrew language, our forefather's name was change by God from Jacob to Israel – meaning "who struggles with God." Jacob was in a desperate situation. He was about to face his brother Esau, whom many years earlier he had cheated out of his inheritance. He went aside from his wives, children and herds the night before meeting Esau and wrestled with a man until daybreak. The man could not overpower Jacob, so he touched his hip socket to dislocate it, yet still he could not prevail. The man insisted that Jacob let him go, but Jacob would not until the man pronounced a blessing upon him. The man changed Jacob's name to Israel, because Jacob had struggled with the Divine and with man and had overcome.

This encounter has been interpreted many ways. Was it God, Himself, who came down to wrestle with Jacob? Was it an angel? Was it an earthly messenger? And what does it mean that Jacob had struggled with God? We know he had struggled with men. How do we struggle with the Divine? First of all, by wondering if there is a Divine. But that question itself is proof that there is. Within us, something reaches to understand that part of Him having been deposited into our beings. To neglect it is to spend our days in futility and to embrace it is to begin our grandest conquest. Who is God and where is He? And how are do relate to the infinite?

Does it seem absurd to ask for forgiveness for not believing when in fact to ask shows our belief? After all, we must think someone is listening to our confession. And so is the heart of mankind; one day believing and the next wavering, yet all in all still believing. Doubt is mixed with faith and sometimes faith with doubt. At times we are free of doubt and others free of faith. And God remains and does not change and we pull ourselves up again to believe in His goodness.

The Jewish people have been scattered throughout the world for millennia. In their wanderings, they have endured hostilities toward themselves and their God. In the late 1800s and early 1900s Russian governmental structures and oppression of the Jews within their borders, helped pave the way to atheism. Being robbed of our Torahs, sacred literature and public worship; meant our faith and our people received generational blows to who we are and what we believe. To be a Jewish atheist seemed the norm throughout the country. However, there is nothing normal about an atheistic Jew. We are the people of the Book. Our history and our continuance are directly connected to the God of Israel. Thankfully, as we come out of oppression, we have the chance to rid ourselves of disbelief.

For the Jewish soul, God is. We may not understand why this is or why He is, but these things remain.

PRAYER
Forgive Me for not Believing in You

Avinu Malkeinu, our Father and our King, forgive our disbelief. We confess our bent to question your existence and involvement in this world and in our lives. We confess our tendencies to look aside to other things and to invent, in our minds, other means and destinies. We renounce all other gods and all forms of men that seek to draw us away in deception. Let us not follow another. Let us not inquire of false gods nor turn to follow their practices.

When we are frail of strength and mind, succor us with your words and cause us to delight in your precepts. Be to us a God of wonder and majesty; a God of sovereignty and dominion. Cause our hearts to incline toward you and to remember all your ways. Awaken us to your presence and encourage us with your light. Be to us a God above all gods and tend the flock of your people Israel; tend us as a shepherd and carry us close to your heart.

O God of Israel, forgive our groanings. Forgive our loathings. When our hearts grow faint within us and we can stand no more, be our comfort and our solid ground. You are our God and we are the people of your pasture. You are our God and we will ever praise you. You are our God and we will ever acknowledge you. Help us, O Lord, to seek your face.
Amein.

INTRODUCTION

Forgive Me for Forgetting to Pray

Why do we pray? Is it for ourselves, others or to please God? Do we truly expect anything from having engaged it? The exercise of praying can be viewed as a monotonous, one-sided conversation. If we aren't much of a conversationalist, even when sitting face to face with another, prayer may seem impossible. It may also seem like nonsense. What are we doing when we pray? Are we placing our orders with God? Does He need help figuring out what we need? Must He be informed of what's going on down here? Is He all about hearing how wondrous He is and what a magnificent job He has done with His creation?

There is no need to inform God of anything. He sees and knows and for every small detail we take to Him, there are undoubtedly many more of which He is aware. He doesn't need our advice. He made all, understands all and is watching over all with all wisdom and knowledge. We don't need to give Him our wish list; He knows what's in our hearts and the things on which our minds dwell. We do need to praise Him and offer our thanksgiving. Not because He a cosmic egotist, but because it changes our perceptions, our attitudes and ultimately our lives. Praise and gratitude, directed to our Creator, lightens our souls and causes us to reunite with what's good in life and reassures that we are not alone.

We pray for ourselves, so we may be changed. We pray for others so they may be changed. In most cases, the action of praying produces an immediate uplift of mind and soul, but medical science agrees that is also can produce greater physical health. Like exercise of the body, exercise of the soul, in prayer, causes healthy hormonal changes, and doctors around the globe agree that if a person prays or is prayed for by another, chances for healing are multiplied.

In Judaism, prayer is an exercise of our awareness of God. We are aware of Him so we approach, and as we approach our awareness increases. Awareness and faith are interchangeable and both are related to the Divine. When we end our time of prayer and go forth into the day, we are changed. We have heightened our sensitivity to the realms beyond us and are assured that heaven was brought down to us as we reached up for it. We have been with God and will carry this union with us.

We praise God for who He is so we may remind ourselves of His nature, and He is pleased when we remember. He desires connection with us and is glad when we acknowledge His position. We also give credit where credit is due. From Him comes our source of life and wellbeing.

A father once asked his son, "When a benefit comes to you, do you think it from the hand of God? Or could is it circumstance?" His budding son replied, "It is from God." The father went on to ask how could he be sure it was from the hand of God. The son replied, "If I credit God, even if it was circumstance, I have praised the One worthy of praise and have done no wrong. If I credit circumstance, when it was God, I have erred and deprived Him of my gratitude. Therefore, I will give thanks to God for all things."

In Jewish prayer, we ask God to give us the things He knows are best. Even when we bring a direct request before Him, we ask that He give according to His perfect knowledge of the situation and what would indeed be a benefit, not a hindrance to us or another. We also confess our sins and in return are forgiven.

PRAYER
Forgive Me for Forgetting to Pray

Avinu Malkeinu, our Father and our King, forgive our busyness and complacency. Forgive our neglect to pray. We confess our selfish tendencies that lead away from you and from focus of mind and heart toward your throne. We have gone our way, seeking other things. We have placed before our eyes that which you have made, yet not given thanks. We have worked at our endeavors without working toward greater awareness. We have not been grateful. We have not praised. We have neglected to pray for ailing brothers and sought the help of other men without seeking your face.

O God, forgive us for our lack of focus upon your greatness, your holiness and your kingship. Forgive us for lack of corporate prayer and for neglecting times of personal praise, request and thanksgiving before you. May we be quick to seek you. May we rise to greet you in the morning and may the last words upon our lips each night come before you. May we pause to recognize you throughout each day and render to you all glory, honor and praise, which are rightfully yours.

Forgive us, O God, for neglecting to seek you. Strengthen our minds to remember your deeds and to give thanks. Strengthen our hearts to thirst for you and our souls to cling to you. Forgive us when we forget to pray and enlighten us to remember.
Amein.

INTRODUCTION

Forgive Me for not holding back my Anger with my Children

As parents, we face the pressures of the world outside our homes then our young pressures inside. Our children are our joy and delight and the quickest inroad to our last ounce of patience. From their positions, we may seem unstable. The same parent that sweeps them up with a hug and multiplied kisses can then snap at them with angry words or over-do a punishment. I believe our true intentions toward our children are loving and kind and the beast inside each one of us does not speak our real words nor perform our real desires. We love our children to the core even when their words or actions are not savory, nor sweet. Parenting tries us to the depths. We are the biggest in the house, but to remain the bigger person in attitude can twist our guts and provoke our wits.

God gave us our children. His intentions were to populate the earth. He was also desirous that we should train our children to know Him, to love and serve Him and to love and deal kindly with their neighbors. As Jewish parents, we instill the words of Torah and other sacred, Jewish writings and the love of heritage and goodwill toward mankind.

When we perform our parental tasks well, we are able to cope with the everyday stresses and strains of childhood illnesses, surprise comments from teachers, sandbox quarrels and permanent marker on the walls in the family room. After all, we are family and it is *our* room. However, when we share that room with guests, we'd just as soon erase some of our family doings. When we are tired, pressed for time, under a load on the job, untangling relational dilemmas or feeling under the weather those little things done by our little ones can unravel us in an instant.

As our children grow into adolescence, we long for the days of the permanent marker and must up our game to stay aware, loving and nurturing. The teenage years bring more challenges and only after we launch our prodigy out into the world do we realize they will still invoke strong emotion when they call at midnight with a heart-ache or emergency room visit with one of our grandchildren. They will always be our children and we will forever be their parents. As marriage is for better or worse, so it is with our children.

When we express our anger toward them it momentarily erases our love, but only for the moment. Then both parties get back on track – usually. When things remain tense with an older or adult child, we must examine the dynamics causing the strain and come forward as parents to make things right. We continue to lead and guide our children for as long as we are in their lives, and hopefully that is for life.

As with any other relationship within Judaism, we are directed to go to the offended party before going to God. There is no need to ask forgiveness of our heavenly father when we have not been a good father or mother. We go to our children then to God. He will freely pardon our parental blunders, yet also require resolution for better interactions and fuller expressions of love and where needed, restitution.

God also understands our parental exasperations, just as any other facet of our existence on this earth. Times of quiet prayer and meditation will help to send us on our way, back to our children and refocused as our best selves.

PRAYER
Forgive Me for not holding back my Anger with my Children

Avinu Malkeniu, our Father and our King, forgive us for expressing anger to our children. Cause us to remember your kindliness toward us as a father caring for his own. Empower us to watch over them with gentleness, to guide them with patience and to respond to them with loving words and deeds. When we are tired and stressed help us to turn our thoughts toward you and immerse ourselves in the calming words of our ancestors and sages. Help us to pause when tempted to react and to seek forgiveness from our children when we have been angry or cruel.

O God, we give thanks to you for our young ones. We give thanks as they age and grow in completeness. May they experience health, happiness and closeness to you, O God, and be surrounded with faithfulness, goodness and love. May they ever seek your face and cling to the words of your Torah. May they find fulfillment and delight and enact good to those around them.

Oh God of our fathers, forgive us when we respond in anger; may it not remain in our generations. May neither grudge nor unforgiveness rule in our posterity. May we be a people of peace that secures peace for our children and their children and theirs after them, dwelling in charity one for another and regarding the wellbeing of others as dear as our own. O God, forgive us for anger directed toward the children you have given and let us recall your goodness and forbearance to all. Amein.

INTRODUCTION

Forgive Me for not being Kind

Kindness is contagious. If we approach a bank teller, cashier or a service clerk with a smile on our face and kindness in our voice, we will most likely be met with the same. If we help someone with their bags, give up our seat on the bus or send a card to someone needing encouragement, we have the instant satisfaction of placing another's interests above our own. The opposite is also true. When we approach with selfish words and intent, are hurried and bothered, pretend we do not see the needs of another or neglect to show concern when we are capable, we will be seen as uncaring and thus unkind.

In Jewish teaching, we are not so much credited with being kind to those who are kind to us, but with kindness toward our enemies, the stranger and the poor. When we are pleasant and caring toward those who cannot repay or do not wish to repay, we have gone beyond ourselves and have accomplished the divine, for God, who is above all and good to all, is kind to us; lowly as we are.

Kindness to those who cannot repay can change the course of someone's day or their entire lives. Kindness to our enemies can soften a hardened heart or produce healthy shame resulting in repentance. When we are kind to the stranger, we extend the hand that was once given to our ancestors when joining Joseph in the land of Goshen. Kindness is always current. We remember the good done to us in times past and live toward the same in the present. Kindness is always in style. When others are too busy, thoughtless or bothered to give a kind word or perform a kind deed; we see how another is encouraged when we pause in their stead.

When we are unkind, we join the ranks of scoundrels, the greedy, the selfish, the reckless and uncaring. Our outward sickness toward mankind reflects an inner sickness of heart and soul. The unkind are unkind to themselves. The Torah teaches that we must love ourselves before loving our neighbors. Ill treatment of others reflects error in loving ourselves. Love begets love; kindness, kindness. If all were kind what a world that would be. If all were thoughtless how would we exist? And so, we cultivate kindness through consideration for what is pleasant and desirable to ourselves and give that to another.

Mother's begin to teach kindness to their children at any early age. They instruct to share their toys and treats and to take turns on the playground, all for the sake of kindness. Why do we need such instruction? In Judaism, we find there are two inclinations in each soul; the good and the evil. The evil inclination naturally attempts to exert itself over our fellow and in fact, over ourselves. We must focus on conquering it as a daily task. When we fail, we make things right with our fellow and with God and try again to master the art of choice – good over evil.

We are not alone in this struggle. Our rabbis and sages teach of the good we may do for the sake of God's name, for our brethren and for the nations. These deeds are referred to as mitzvot or good deeds performed outside of ourselves; for the good of others. However, the word actually means *commands*. Thus, we do the commands that befit another and speak of the kindness and goodness of God.

PRAYER
Forgive Me for not being Kind

Avinu Makeinu, our Father and our King, forgive our lack of kindness. Forgive our thoughtless acts and careless words. Forgive our pride and impudence toward others. Forgive us when we withhold kindness.

Help to act with obedience to your commands and with willing hearts to regard your Torah. As we were once strangers in the land of Egypt, yet were looked upon with favor as we joined our ancestor, help us to regard the stranger with respect and concern and do good to him as we are able. As there have been poor and needy among us, widows and orphans and those who would seek our help; help us to extend our arms with regard for the weak and our hands in deeds of kindness.

Bring to our remembrance your many kindnesses to your people and to all that your hands have made. Cause us to likewise show kindness and to teach kindness to our children, that they may also cause regard for your name among the nations. Help us to look with favor upon the cause of our brethren and to give freely without restraint when entreated.

O God, forgive us for our lack of empathy, sympathy and kind regard for the frail, the feeble, those without strength and those who cannot entreat. Imbue us with understanding and bless us with ability to be kind to all and give to all even as you have given. Forgive us for our lack and lead us to your mitzvot.
Amein.

INTRODUCTION

Forgive Me for Talking about my Friends

The proverbs of King Solomon speak of a friend that stays closer than a brother, that wounds from a friend can be trusted, that a friend loves at all times and the righteous take caution in friendship. Solomon also said that two are better than one because they have a good return for their labor, and if one falls down he can be picked up by the other. And if two lie down together, they will be warm, but one cannot keep warm alone.

The Tanakh has much to say about friendship. It also speaks of ways friends separate. One of those ways is through gossip. It's a terrible thing to lose a trusted friend. We may have shared our most personal ideas, struggles, mistakes and victories with someone we regarded as our confidant, only to find that our words were poured into the streets or told selectively to those who would use them against us.

The Talmud tells us - that which is hateful to you; do not do to your brother. What are the things we see as hateful? If we were to make a list, then measure our acquaintances by that standard, we may be surprised to find how few of them would make good friends. If we put our friends to such a test, we may discover that we are not as close as previously thought. When people we keep at a distance do to us as we would not do to them, we are not surprised and tolerate the reality of the distance between us. However, when someone we have welcomed into our inner circle treats us as we would not treat them, we are left with pain and dismay; our vulnerability being laid bare before others.

When we speak of others, behind their backs as the saying goes, we may ruin our relationship along with our reputation. It may be spoken, behind our backs, that we are talebearers, untrustworthy or slanderers. The tongue speaks life and death. It can elevate a person to a place of healing and self-worth or dash to pieces in an instant. Solomon said when we talk a lot, sin is will happen. So the wise will refrain from talking too much.

At times, talking too long to the same person over the phone, at lunch or on a drive across town; can set us up for saying too much. Perhaps we didn't mean to tell a thing about another or didn't realize the other party was about to bring up a matter. Then it happens and we're caught in a web that can go forth at lightning speed. The rabbis tell a story about this spread of gossip.

Our words go out as feathers in the wind. Once they are gone, they cannot be retrieved. Imagine trying to gather up just one hundred feathers. We may successfully stuff the majority of them back into our bags, yet even one that gets away is carried to unknown places. The same occurs with our words. Once they leave our lips, they cannot be retracted. Even if we apologize, the words will linger in the mind of the injured.

King Solomon also said an offended brother is harder to win than a city. How can this be? Can we destroy a relationship with a single offense? Will it take several? How can we know since we are not able to perceive our brother's heart? If we love someone, should we push the limits? A focus upon our words is in order. Perhaps speaking less or not to certain people is needed. Our words can hurt, yet also heal. Let's determine to speak well of our friends even as we would have them speak to us. After all, these are our friends not foes.

PRAYER
Forgive Me for Talking about my Friends

Avinu Malkeinu, our Father and our King, forgive us for the misuse of our words. We confess speaking to those we should not. We confess engaging conversations we should not. We have sinned with our lips and injured with our tongues. Help us to guard the honor of our friends as we would our own and as we would have them do. Help us to feel the prick of conscious when we would open our mouths to slander, insult or betray a trust.

May we be true, loyal, faithful and sure to those within our circles and may the friend of our bosom find rest and confidence. May we be to others as we would have them to ourselves and may we treat all men with respect and guarded tongue.

O God, our God, forgive the sins of our mouths. Forgive the sins of our wandering tongues. Cause us to be silent when our words could injure and give us courage to speak with regard for the one who is slandered, insulted or belittled. May the words of our mouths and the meditations of our hearts be acceptable. Forgive us for speaking ill of our friends and listening to ill spoken of them. Amein.

INTRODUCTION

Forgive Me for thinking negative thoughts about my

Mother-In-Law

There are many jokes and stories about the faulty relationship between mother-in-law and son-in-law. She's always butting into her daughter's marriage, she comes and stays, she disregards the virtues of her son-in-law and is in general – a trouble maker he could do without. There's also the mother-in-law who will not be convinced that her daughter-in-law is good enough for her son. After all, she was the woman in his life for many years and she developed a strong bond with him through serving and tending him as most moms do. Either way, the son-in-law or daughter-in-law may feel put down and disregarded. These feelings can escalate until a rift occurs in the family and relationships are strained or dissolved.

As with any relationship, the one with our mother-in-laws can build in trust and appreciation or erode with unkind words and alienation. It is not true to say if we do our part she will positively respond. However, it is good to try. Ultimately, the relationship is dependent upon three; the mother, her son or daughter and the one who married into the family. The son or daughter can feel caught in the middle of holiday feuds and weekend visits. His or her spouse may feel helpless and hopeless to be accepted.

The truth is that extended family is important just as blood relatives. The mother-in-law and daughter-in-law both love the same man and desire life's best for him. The mother-in-law and the son-in-law love the same woman and desire her best. The love each has for the other is different, but none the less of utmost importance to the peace and functioning of the family. If we made love-teams, that is; mom-in-law and daughter-in-law team up to love the man in the middle and mom-in-law and son-in-law team for the good of the lady between them, perhaps things could run more smoothly.

In Judaism, our children and grandchildren, which carry out our heritage and destiny, are prized and cherished parts of a whole nation of people. We teach and train them, pray for them and set examples before them to be good Jews, good citizens and good family. However, what we truly want is great family. We want the generational connection to who we are and where we came from to be the tie that binds. When we learn to love the in-laws, we are set to share our young.

When we harbor negative thoughts about our mother-in-laws, we harbor negative about our spouses. This is the woman who raised the one closest to us. If we think she did a less than satisfactory job, we may think so by observing the actions, habits and demeanors of the child she taught and we married. Do we think our way is better than hers and theirs? Perhaps it is but maybe not. Sometimes time will tell and until then, team-loving and forgiveness is in order.

It is helpful to choose one or two things about our mother-in-laws for which we are grateful; if we find those same traits in our spouses, all the better. Thoughts of gratitude can replace ones that put down and critique. She is the one who brought our beloved into the world; if we can but dwell on that one virtue we would do good. When we find ourselves unable to keep a reign on our thoughts, we should step out and perform a deed of kindness to our spouses' mother and even their fathers. Blending a family takes concentration, but the rewards go beyond the lives of just two and the here and now.

PRAYER
Forgive Me for thinking negative thoughts about my
Mother-In-Law

Avinu Malkeinu, our Father and our King, forgive us for harboring ill toward our mother-in-laws. We confess our negative thoughts, our contempt, our sorrow and anger. We confess our bitter words and deeds and our spite that has brought injury to our spouses and their parents.

Help us, O God, to consider each member of our families and our spouses' families as unique, worthy, goodly and due our heartfelt respect. Help us to replace our negative thoughts with ones that uplift within and practice kindness without. Help us to desist from causing pressure upon our spouse with our attitudes and help us regard each member as a team for which we will strive to win.

O God, forgive our inner complaints, let them not rule over us and not take form from without us. Cause us to be bearers of love and goodwill, kindness and respect and unity above all things. May we be the healing balm in our spouses' families and engineers of peace among our brethren. Forgive us when we meditate upon our mother-in-laws with ill will and disdain. Forgive for the sake our spouses and children and all that would look upon our generations.
Amein.

INTRODUCTION

Help Me to Remember Jerusalem

No topic on Jewish prayer would be complete without dialogue concerning Jerusalem. King David said to pray for the peace of Jerusalem and those that do will be secure and prosper. When it came to this great city, he went so far as to call down a curse upon his body; upon his right hand and his tongue. "If I forget you, O Jerusalem, may my right hand forget its skill. May my tongue cling to my palate, if I do not remember you, if I do not bring up Jerusalem at the beginning of my joy" (Psalms 137:5-6).

David was a songwriter, psalmist and musician. His right hand penned beautiful words and stroked the harp in such a way that King Saul was relieved of an evil spirit when David played for him. David had been a shepherd boy. He had killed a lion and a bear when they came to attack his family's flocks and he slew an enemy of Israel with the swing of his slingshot. His hands were weapons and writers of wisdom, reflection and faith.

David was a zealous man. He knew when to fight and when to beseech the God of Israel with tears. He was an honest soul whose words have been recited time and again for millennia. He was a man after God's own heart and from his heart came the beauty of a melodic tongue and a skillful hand.

In the book of II Samuel, in the Tanakh, we see that David and his men took Jerusalem from the Jebusites. He bought a threshing floor and oxen, built and alter and sacrificed to the God of Israel on what is now known as the Temple Mount. He relocated his people there and by the tenth century B.C.E. the presence of the Israelites was strong in number and influence. David's son Solomon built the Temple of God on the same site that his father had sacrificed to God – Mt. Moriah. Historical and Archeological evidence support these words of the Bible.

The ownership of Jerusalem has changed hands and is the center of controversy. Yet, for the Jew, the words of David ring in our ears as does his desire in our hearts to keep Jerusalem an eternal focal point. David had strong and skillful hands. He had used them in behalf of his family, his people and his God. He was so inclined toward Jerusalem as the City of David that he called down a curse on himself; if he ever forgot her. If I forget thee, O Jerusalem, may my right hand forget its skill and may my tongue cling to the roof of my mouth. May I not be able to write, speak or sing.

Today's Jewish people are divided on the subject in reality, but not in heart. We know Jerusalem is part of our history, heritage and dialogue within ourselves and with each other. We don't forget, but sometimes we do not know how to remember her. Few would call down a curse upon their right hands if she slipped from their minds or pronounce judgment on their tongues. However, the words of King David, our ancestor, are well recorded in conscious. Although we may not agree with how or what to pray concerning her, we do pray and we do love her. When we visit the State of Israel, a stop off in the great city is always a highlight and its wailing-wall, or place of Jewish prayer, is a reminder of what we once had. We pray there and wish there. We write notes to God and insert them in the crevices between the massive stones. We walk away somehow feeling closer to Him, heard by Him and knowing we have just done a very ancient, communal and sacred act.

PRAYER
Help Me to Remember Jerusalem

O God of our fathers, God of Abraham, Isaac and Jacob, God of Israel, hear our prayer for your holy city; the place that bears your name. For the sake of our brothers and our friends, we pray for peace. For the sake of our ancestors who walked the Temple courts, for the sake of David, our great king, for the sake of our posterity, we ask for peace.

Forgive us O God, when we forget your city, when are go about our own ways and do not keep our past and our history before us. Forgive us when we disregard your words concerning our people and we do not look to you regarding your will for the nations. Forgive us when we forget. Help us to recall the ancient stones of Jerusalem. Help us to care for her, love her, pray for her and seek her.

May she be as dear to us as she was to our great king in days of old. May we regard her among our highest joys and do good to her and those within her gates. We pray for the peace of Jerusalem and entreat you, O God, to bring it soon.
Amein.

INTRODUCTION

Help Me to Remember Mashiach

Last, but far from least in Jewish prayer, is the hope of the Messiah, or Mashiach as is said in Hebrew. We desire liberation from a worldly system that does not allow us to worship our God in freedom. We wish for peace, rest, perfect health and the restoration of all things as God promised. We know when the Messiah comes, He will liberate us from oppression and set the world aright. He will descend from the line of David, gather our people back to the Land of Israel and build the third Temple in Jerusalem. He will bring justice and end all hatred, evil and wickedness. He will restore the sacrificial system and re-estate the Jewish courts.

Throughout the ages, the Messiah was seen as an individual coming from God. In more modern times, thoughts have swayed to a Messianic age rather than a being; a time of peace, rest and perfection when there is no need for fear and the lion will lay down with the lamb. There will be nothing to antagonize or alarm and nothing that is not in its best state of being. Will this time or person ever come? The answer is yes.

The Messiah was promised to Israel. Although we do not see him specifically in the Torah, perhaps because the focus was on the inauguration and early history of our people, we see him throughout the words of our prophets. The term "Mashiach or Messiah" means anointed one. The one anointed by the God of Israel to rule the earth with goodness and harmony.

If this Mashiach is sent from God, Himself, and is so desired as the one who will right the wrongs of mankind, how can we forget him? How do we forget about anything? We get busy, we lose focus, we don't stay connected to the text that reminds or to the people who wait along with us. Waiting also cause us to forget. What is our response when we have waited and waited for something and it does not arrive?

Our children cannot wait for their birthdays or a holiday. We can't wait until vacation or until we close on our new home. We can't wait to see relatives, to view a movie or to attend a concert. However, we do wait. Sometimes we wait with excitement and at others with quiet resolve because we know exactly when the wait will end. Waiting for the Messiah is akin to waiting for the birth of a child. We know the child is coming, we have an approximate idea of when, but we cannot speak of date and time.

The Mashiach is coming, this we know, and we may speculate as to when, but we cannot be certain. We attempt to read the signs. We search the prophets, if we are brave, and look about us to see if there is an alignment between their words and the state of world affairs. We dare to hope. We've been waiting for centuries. He will come. Our God does not lie. We will continue to wait and we will not be disappointed.

PRAYER
Help Me Remember Mashiach

Avinu Malkeinu, our Father and our King, forgive us for forgetting your promises. You have been faithful to us from the beginning, bearing with us and surrounding us with your unfailing love. You are worthy of trust and adoration for your words are sure and your acts just. You will never forsake us.

Forgive us, O God, when we lay aside your laws, when we disregard your percepts and turn away our confidence. You alone are for us; you alone are our God. We have none other. Your words are true and your promises certain. We place our hope in you. We long for the day when you will regather us and make our lot secure. We yearn for times of refreshing and the cessation of all that makes afraid. We sit in silence before you, you alone sustain our souls.

We ask for the Mashaich, we entreat you that he draws near. We confess our lethargy and depression as we wait. Cause us to rise in hope and thanksgiving. Cause us to hear the sound of his coming and to see with our eyes the rebuilding of our Holy Temple and the restoration of your Law. May we live in peace under his rulership and in him find peace for our souls. May we be at ease as his subjects with none to harass or intimidate.

O God of our fathers, enliven as we wait. Hear our cries and answer. Lift our countenance as we look to you, for you alone can gladden the heart and revive the soul. Put within us your hope as we cling to you. Forgive us when we accuse you. Forgive us when we do not believe. Send to us Mashiach, speedily and soon. May the entire house of Israel rejoice and may we see him in our days.
Amein.

Dear Reader,

If you enjoyed this book or found it useful, I would be very grateful if you would post a short review on Amazon. Your support really does make a difference and I read all the reviews personally so I can get your feedback and make this book even better.

If you would like to leave a review, all you need to do is click the review link on this book's Amazon page here.

If you are a member of kindleunlimited, I would be most grateful if you would scroll to the back of the book so I will be paid for your borrowed book.

Thanks again for your support.

America Selby

Please leave a review

Go to amazon.com and type in America Selby to find my books.

CPSIA information can be obtained
at www.ICGtesting.com
Printed in the USA
LVHW082142250123
737973LV00029B/908

9 781539 127192